WITHDRAWN

W9-BEK-396

INSTITUTE OF TECHNOLOGY
SAVAGE LIBRARY

Children
from Australia to
Zimbabwe

BEVERLY GREENWOOD
SCHOOL LIBRARY

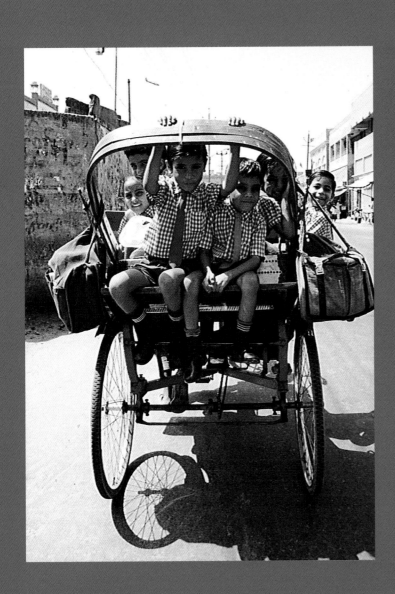

Children from

Australia to Zimbabwe

A Photographic Journey around the World

Maya Ajmera & Anna Rhesa Versola

with a foreword by Marian Wright Edelman

SHAKTI for Children
Charlesbridge

Foreword

I have had the good fortune to meet children of many countries on four continents—Asia, North America, Europe, and Africa. As you will see when you read *Children from Australia to Zimbabwe: A Photographic Journey around the World,* some of these children lead very different lives from yours or mine. Some wear traditional clothing woven in bright colors by their mothers. Some live in houses made not from bricks or wood but from mud or grasses. Many speak languages that you and I wouldn't understand.

But children the world over share many things in common:

All children play. Playing is how very young children learn and explore. Although their toys and games might look quite different, you would be surprised to see how familiar child-play is. Remember banging a spoon against a pot, making kitchen "music" while your mother cooked dinner? Across the world, children learn about sound in similar ways.

All children need their families. No matter where he or she lives, nothing is more important in a child's life than a loving family that takes good care of their child.

All children share other basic needs that must be met. Each child needs and deserves healthy food, clothing, shelter, health care, education, and safety from violence and war.

All children need and deserve a livable earth, breathable air, and drinkable water. We adults have to make sure the planet we leave behind is in good shape to support our children and their children.

All children need and deserve the nurturing and protection of communities and governments. Families do not raise children in a vacuum. Children need communities and governments that help support families, rather than make it harder to bring up children.

All children can contribute to society. Each child has something to give that will make this world a better place, if we adults ensure that he or she gets the chance to give it.

Children are a mighty force. The fate of humankind is in your hands. Learn about the heroes and heroines of your nation and other nations and cultures. And, please, learn from the mistakes my generation and those before it have made. Remember: Hatred can only destroy, while love and appreciation of one another fortify the world.

When I was a young woman, a fellowship enabled me to spend a summer in what was then called the Soviet Union. Exploring this very different place made me see that I wasn't just an individual—I was also part of a worldwide community. My actions, my accomplishments, my failures could affect people and places beyond my immediate family, friends, neighborhood, state, and nation.

I hope you will think more about that idea. Today we truly live in a global village, connected across continents by television, high-speed travel, and the Internet. Your choices and your actions will be felt worldwide, by today's and tomorrow's children. You can be a positive or negative force in the world.

I also hope that you will keep in mind one additional similarity that you share with all of the earth's children. I hope it will help you embrace rather than push away those who look or speak or dress or think differently than you do:

All children are gifts of God.

—MARIAN WRIGHT EDELMAN
President, Children's Defense Fund

Inside this book, you will read about these countries and the children who live in them.

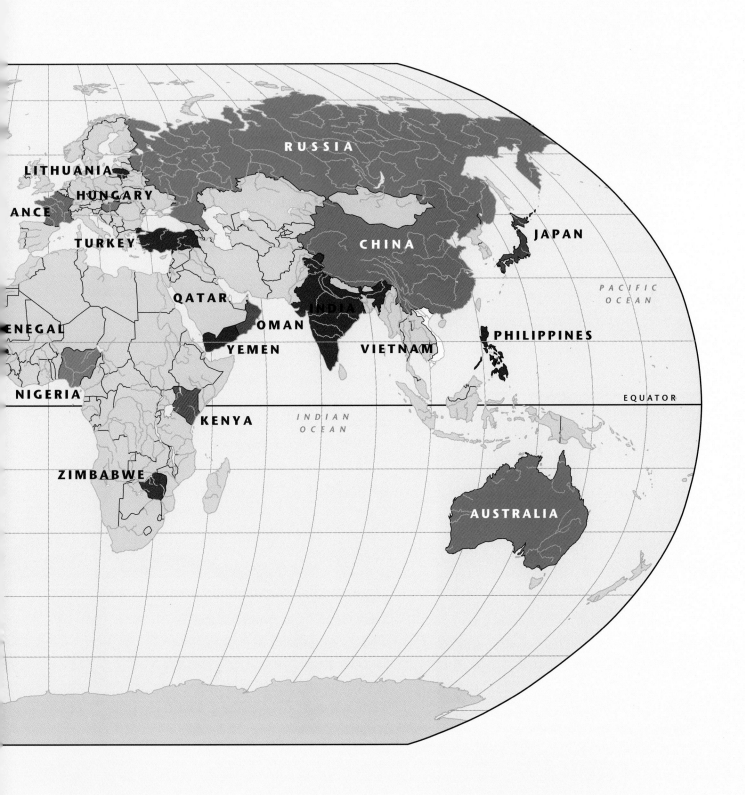

LITHUANIA

HUNGARY

ANCE

TURKEY

RUSSIA

CHINA

JAPAN

PACIFIC
OCEAN

QATAR

OMAN

YEMEN

INDIA

VIETNAM

PHILIPPINES

ENEGAL

NIGERIA

KENYA

INDIAN
OCEAN

EQUATOR

ZIMBABWE

AUSTRALIA

Good Day from Australia

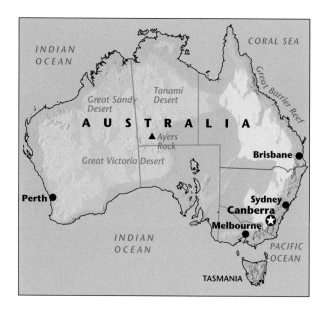

AUSTRALIA is both a continent and a country. It is the sixth largest country in the world, and the smallest continent. Large areas of Australia are desert, where it is flat and very dry. Almost in the middle of the country is a huge rock the size of a mountain, called Ayers Rock. There are caves in the rock that are decorated with paintings and carvings left by the first people to live in Australia—the Aborigines.

Aborigines were once nomadic and traveled from place to place to hunt and gather food that grew in the wild. Their hunting weapons were boomerangs, and their hunting dogs were dingoes, a kind of dog that once lived only in Australia. Dingoes like to howl and hunt in packs, like wolves.

Today many different people live in Australia. Some of them are the great-great-grandchildren of people who came here from countries in Europe. The girls on the opposite page are at a beach festival in Perth, waving flags from Great Britain and Australia. The people who have settled more recently come from other countries, like China and the Philippines, Vietnam, or Malaysia. The girl who is dancing here is from Indonesia.

This is the first day of school for the two young friends you see on the left. They wear uniforms to their classes. Some children do not go to regular schools because they live in

a place called the Outback, far away from the big cities. They can wear what they want because their teachers cannot see them. These students attend "schools of the air" and use two-way radios to talk with their teachers about their lessons.

More facts about Australia

Capital: Canberra
Languages: English and Aboriginal languages
Total Population: 17,900,000
Number of Children: 4,100,000
Favorite Sports: Cricket, rugby, and soccer (also called football)
Environmental Fact: The sun is very strong in Australia, and all children are encouraged to "slip, slop, and slap"—slip on a shirt, slop on some sunscreen, and slap on a hat.

Other "A" Countries: Afghanistan, Albania, Algeria, Andorra, Angola, Antigua and Barbuda, Argentina, Armenia, Austria, and Azerbaijan

Oi (OYEE) from Brazil

Brazil is the biggest country in South America. Once it was mostly rain forest. Now it has many large orange groves, cattle ranches, and coffee plantations. In São Paulo, near the coast, factories are busy making cars and other products. So the children of Brazil, like children in many other countries, see things changing all around them, whether they live in the cities or the country, whether their families work and prosper, or struggle to make a living.

Long ago the only way to travel across the rain forest was by boat along the Amazon River, the second-longest river in the world. Today the river is still used like a water highway. But many roads are being built, too, to make travel easier.

Most of the old rain forest still stands, and people are exploring ways to save it. People new to the rain forest can learn a lot about it from the Indians who live there, like the two Kayapo boys on the next page, who are all dressed up for a special occasion. The Indians can tell you which trees have the best nuts and which leaves, or seeds, or bark make good medicines.

Many Africans came to Brazil to work on the sugar plantations. They brought their music with them, and over the years Brazilians have blended the music of Africa and Europe and the Amazon to make their famous dance music, like the samba.

Children often stay up late with the grown-ups, especially during the big annual festival of Carnaval. Like grown-ups, they too can perform a Carnaval dance and beat out rhythms on their conga drums.

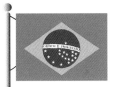

More facts about Brazil

Capital: Brasília

Languages: Portuguese, Spanish, English, French, and languages of the Amazon region

Total Population: 159,100,000

Number of Children: 55,400,000

Favorite Sport: Soccer

Environmental Fact: Brazil makes most of the world's orange juice.

Other "B" Countries: Bahamas, Bahrain, Bangladesh, Barbados, Belarus, Belgium, Belize, Benin, Bhutan, Bolivia, Bosnia and Herzegovina, Botswana, Brunei, Bulgaria, Burkina Faso, Burma (also called Myanmar), and Burundi

你 好 (KNEE-HOW) from China

CHINA has more people living in it than any other country in the world. A Chinese child from the north of the country will have a very different life and a different way of speaking from someone who lives in the wide grasslands of west China or in the warm south.

The young boy on the next page carries a basket of coal as part of his chores at school in Gansu Province, in north central China. Winters there are long and cold, so people burn coal to keep themselves warm.

The Chinese were the first people to use coal as a source of fuel and energy. They were also the first people to make firecrackers for their celebrations. And they invented a way to print letters on paper.

The girls pictured on the next page are from Xinjiang Province, and they are reading prayer books. The Chinese do not use an alphabet for sounding out words, as we do. They use symbols that represent a single word or idea. If you do not speak the same dialect as other people, it does not matter. You can write down your idea in symbols, and they will understand.

Two-humped camels are still used today to travel across remote provinces. A more modern way to travel the long distances between China's big cities is by train.

The most popular means of transport, however, is the bicycle. City streets swarm with bicycles as people travel to work or on errands across town. If you were a child in China, you would no doubt dream of riding a bicycle as soon as you were able and hope one day to have one of your own.

More facts about China

Capital: Beijing

Languages: Mandarin Chinese and other Asian languages

Total Population: 1,208,800,000

Number of Children: 340,400,000

Favorite Sports: Badminton, basketball, soccer, and table tennis

Environmental Fact: Adult giant pandas weigh about 220 pounds. They eat mostly bamboo leaves and shoots and live in the forests of central China near Tibet.

Other "C" Countries: Cambodia, Cameroon, Canada, Cape Verde, Central African Republic, Chad, Chile, Colombia, Comoros, Congo (Democratic Republic of), Congo (Republic of), Costa Rica, Côte d'Ivoire, Croatia, Cuba, Cyprus, and Czech Republic

Hola (O-LA) from the

Dominican Republic

Iᴛ you look at a map, you will see several large islands in the Caribbean Sea. One of them is Hispaniola, and it is divided into two countries: Haiti and the Dominican Republic. The Dominican Republic has the highest mountains in the Caribbean, and a lighthouse that people say can be seen from the moon.

Dominicans are a mixture of peoples, as you can see from the photographs. "We are a sancocho," the Dominicans often say, referring to a favorite dish of the people, which is made from many different meats and vegetables all stewed together in a big pot.

In the Dominican Republic, you can taste the history of the people who have lived there. The plants that the Indians ate long ago were corn, sweet potatoes, peppers, peanuts, and yucca (sometimes called cassava). Dominicans also love a hearty meat stew, which mixes elements from

Spain and Africa. And they eat plantain, a kind of large banana, cooked in different ways, ripe or green, mashed or sliced, boiled, roasted, or fried.

Sugarcane is the Dominican Republic's main

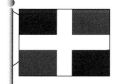

crop, and the country makes and sells refined sugar to the rest of the world. Chopping down sugarcane is hard work, but sometimes even children are called in to help harvest the cane.

City children must often work, too, to bring in a little money for the family. Over half the people in the Dominican Republic live and work in cities. For fun, they play or watch baseball. Dominican baseball players are among the best in the world. And when the game's over, they can get together and dance the merengue, a dance that was invented in the Dominican Republic.

More facts about the Dominican Republic

Capital: Santo Domingo
Language: Spanish
Total Population: 7,700,000
Number of Children: 2,900,000
Favorite Sports: Baseball, basketball, soccer, and volleyball
Environmental Fact: Over four thousand humpback whales that live in the North Atlantic Ocean come to the northern coast of the Dominican Republic to have babies.

Other "D" Countries: Denmark, Djibouti, and Dominica

Hola from Ecuador

ECUADOR means "equator" in Spanish. If you look at a map of the world, you can see a line drawn across the middle of it. This is the equator. It runs right through Ecuador, which is how the country got its name. Ecuador stretches from the Galápagos Islands, over the high Andes Mountains, to the rain forest of the Amazon.

Most of the people in Ecuador are American Indians, who have lived here since ancient times. But over four hundred years ago, people began to arrive from Spain and Africa and settled here. Now almost everyone grows up speaking Spanish, going to church, and taking part in Christian festivals that remember important events in the life of Jesus, like Easter and Christmas.

Most Ecuadorans live in cities in the highlands and along the coast. The easiest way to get from one town to another is by bus. There are a lot of them plying the highways, and bus tickets are cheap. Some of the roads and paths across the mountains, however, are too steep and narrow for cars or buses. So the people who live and farm there use horses and donkeys to help them carry heavy packs of wood, fruits, vegetables, and goods to the town markets. A child can drive a donkey along a road as well as a grown-up.

On the next page, a young girl is selling handwoven woolen rugs at the famous market in Otavalo. Saturday is the busiest day, and the local people arrive early to fill their stalls with handmade rugs, sweaters, and carvings to sell to visitors.

If you wanted to buy bread or medicines or groceries, you would go to a store in town. The

front steps of a shop make a comfortable spot for these girls reading their schoolbooks.

More facts about Ecuador

Capital: Quito

Languages: Spanish and Amerindian languages like Quechua

Total Population: 11,200,000

Number of Children: 4,400,000

Favorite Sport: Soccer

Environmental Fact: The Galápagos Islands are home to several animal species found nowhere else in the world, such as one species of the giant tortoise. These tortoises can grow to be four feet long and are like large turtles, except they live on land and not in water.

Other "E" Countries: Egypt, El Salvador, Equatorial Guinea, Eritrea, Estonia, and Ethiopia

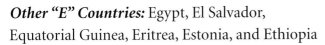

Bonjour (BON-ZHOOR) from France

FRANCE is not the only country where people speak French. You can hear French spoken in places as far apart as Vietnam and Senegal and Canada. If a French child meets a child from one of those countries and does not know the other languages spoken there, they can always talk to each other in French.

French children today learn in school about the days long ago when France had kings and queens. They learn about the many famous French artists and scientists, and about the beautiful palaces and cathedrals of their country. People come from far and wide to visit the old French cities. But France is famous, too, for everyday things that children learn about at home, or on the farm, or in their hometown.

If you lived there, you could find out what it is like to be a bridesmaid or a page at the wedding of a relative, like the children in the top photograph on the next page.

If you went to the bakery to buy bread for your family, you would most probably bring home long, thin, crusty loaves of white bread, like the girl with the bicycle. They are called baguettes, and you find them all over France.

If you like cheese, there are over four hundred different kinds to choose from. Perhaps your family owns a farm with dairy cows or goats, and you make your own cheese to enjoy at home and to sell.

Perhaps your family has a vineyard and grows grapes that will be crushed and made into wine. As a child in such a place, you would grow up hearing the adults around you talk about the weather and seasons and soil and the prices they

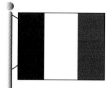

can get for selling grapes or wine. You would know more about how wine is made than someone who just goes and buys it from a store.

More facts about France

Capital: Paris
Language: French
Total Population: 57,000,000
Number of Children: 12,200,000
Favorite Sports: Cycling and soccer
Environmental Fact: The highest mountain in Europe is Mont Blanc, which means "white mountain." It is always covered in snow, which makes it popular among skiers.

Other "F" Countries: Fiji and Finland

Hola from Guatemala

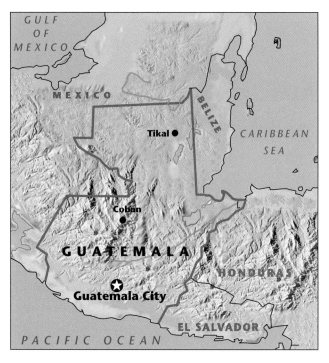

Guatemala is a country of volcanoes and earthquakes. Earthquakes have destroyed Guatemala City twice in the last hundred years, but each time the city has been rebuilt, and now it is the largest city in Central America, with more than two million people living in it.

Almost half the people living in Guatemala today are children, and many of them live in cities and towns. If your family does not have much money, you most likely will not spend much time in school. Instead, you will stay at home and help your parents. If you are too little to do grown-up work, you can look after younger brothers and sisters and help with chores.

Many children live in the highlands that stretch across most of the country. They help on the family farm, growing vegetables for themselves and to sell in the markets in town.

Most Guatemalans are descendants of the Maya Indians, who lived here long before the Spanish came, hoping to find gold and staying to rule the country. Guatemalans learned Spanish and Christianity from their rulers and from the Spanish priests who came here with them.

Five hundred years ago, before the Spanish arrived, the local people were weaving fine wool fabric using natural dyes. As you can see from the photographs, children often wear a modern version, woven in brightly colored stripes. The country is famous for its fabric. You can buy it in the market in Guatemala City or in shops all over the world.

Guatemala also has a vast rain forest. It attracts visitors from other countries, who come

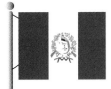

to see its rare birds, plants, and animals. For young Guatemalans, who could work there one day as guides, rangers, or scientists, the rain forest is an important part of their small country's future.

More facts about Guatemala

Capital: Guatemala City

Languages: Spanish and Maya languages

Total Population: 10,300,000

Number of Children: 4,800,000

Favorite Sport: Soccer

Environmental Fact: The national bird is the quetzal. Known for its beauty, it is bright green with a red chest, a yellow beak, and a tail that can grow to be over a foot long.

Other "G" Countries: Gabon, The Gambia, Georgia, Germany, Ghana, Greece, Grenada, Guinea, Guinea-Bissau, and Guyana

Szia (SEE-YA) from Hungary

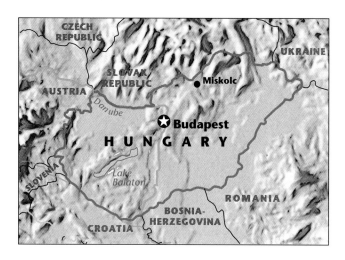

H UNGARY lies in the heart of Europe, far from the sea. The great river Danube marks the northeast border of the country and then turns and flows right down the middle of it, cutting it in two. The Danube also splits the capital city, Budapest. One side of the city is called Buda, and the other is called Pest.

Hungarian children learn early about thermal springs. These are sources of natural hot water, flowing from the ground. There are over five hundred of them. The water is full of minerals that people say are good for you. You can take long, relaxing baths in it, or drink it, and if you were sick, you would feel much better.

Hungary is home to Magyar people as well as Gypsies. "Gypsies" is the common English name for this people, but "Roma" is what they call themselves. The Roma are travelers. They like to stay in a place for a while, doing odd jobs, playing music in cafés, selling baskets, or fixing things for people. Then they like to move on. The girl holding the baby in the picture is a Rom.

In one of these photographs you can see some boys in their music class learning how to play horns and trumpets. Hungarian children can be proud that some of the biggest names in classical music, like Franz Liszt and Béla Bartók, came from their country.

The girl standing in front of the vegetable stand is shopping for peppers. Fields and fields of sweet red peppers grow in the Hungarian countryside. Some are picked and dried and then ground into a spice called paprika that people use all over the world to flavor food like

sausage or stew. Paprika has a special place of honor in the Spice Pepper Museum in the town of Kalocsa.

More facts about Hungary

Capital: Budapest

Language: Hungarian

Total Population: 10,200,000

Number of Children: 2,000,000

Favorite Sports: Soccer and swimming

Environmental Fact: Lake Balaton is the largest freshwater lake in central Europe, and it averages only ten feet deep. It's a favorite spot for people and for many kinds of birds.

Other "H" Countries: Haiti and Honduras

नमस्ते (NA-MA-STAY) from India

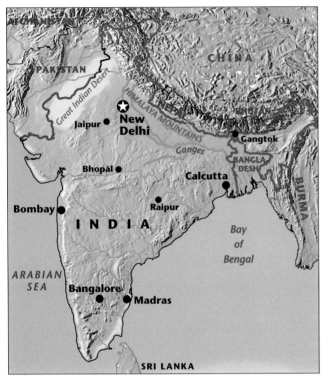

INDIA is a country of opposites. It has the highest mountains in the world—the Himalayas—and land so low that it often floods. There is snow in the north and tropical forest in the south. There are deserts, and there are places where four hundred inches of rain fall every year. Calcutta is one of the world's largest cities, but most Indians live in small villages.

In the cities, among all the other noises, you will hear the creaking of rickshaws. A rickshaw is a two-wheeled cart attached to a bicycle. The children you see riding together in the back of a rickshaw are on their way to school in Jaipur.

It can get very hot in India. People use umbrellas to shield themselves from the sun and enjoy long, cool drinks, like the boy in the photo.

The boys sitting cross-legged on the grass are from Gangtok, in the Himalayas. They are students at a Buddhist temple and are now old enough to wear the colored robes of monks and to shave their heads and to learn about their religion. You can see a heap of brass candle holders scattered on the grass in front of them.

Most people in India belong to the Hindu religion, which honors many gods and goddesses. Each one stands for a different thing. The god called Ganesh is the god of wisdom, and Lakshmi is the goddess of luck.

One thing that Indians share is a love for spices in their food. Some spices are hot, like pepper and ginger. Others are sweet, like cinnamon, or mellow, like cumin. Depending on where you live, you could sit down to a meal of hot curried vegetables with rice and yogurt, or crispy deep-fried pastries, or flat bread and lentils.

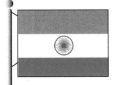

More facts about India

Capital: New Delhi

Languages: Hindi, English, and 14 other official languages

Total Population: 918,600,000

Number of Children: 344,500,000

Favorite Sports: Badminton, cricket, and soccer

Environmental Fact: Children of the Himalaya Mountains play a game called chipko to save trees. One child is given an ax and pretends to chop the tree down. The other children run to the tree and hug it. *Chipko* means "to hug" in Hindi.

Other "I" Countries: Iceland, Indonesia, Iran, Iraq, Ireland, Israel, and Italy

今日は (KEN-NICHI-WON) from Japan

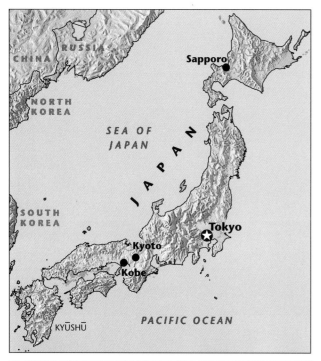

JAPAN is unusual among the countries in this book because most of its people share the same roots and speak the same language. The country is actually a string of four large islands and about four thousand smaller ones and was not easy to reach in olden times. For centuries Japan was more or less on its own. These were the years of the fierce samurai warriors and their leaders, the shoguns.

Japan is now a country with factories that build everything from cars to computers to television sets. Japanese fishing ships are large and fast and catch more fish than most of the other countries in the world.

But the Japanese have not forgotten their past. Many old traditions live on. People have a lot of respect for their parents and older people. You would always try hard to do what your grandmother or grandfather wanted you to do.

On special occasions, girls and women dress up in kimonos, like the little girl in the photo. Boys and men—like the four boys in the photograph—can also wear traditional robes, but theirs are called yukatas. And everyone drinks tea. It is not easy to learn how to prepare and serve it gracefully, in the traditional Japanese way.

One popular art among the Japanese is origami, the art of folding paper into shapes—birds, animals, little cups, or boxes. A favorite shape is the crane, a bird that is sacred in Japan. People believe that if you fold one thousand paper cranes, your wish will come true.

A children's monument honors the legend of a crane that lived for a thousand years. You can

find it in Hiroshima, a city that was bombed in the Second World War, in a place called Peace Memorial Park. The monument is decorated with thousands of paper cranes left there by visitors.

More facts about Japan

Capital: Tokyo
Language: Japanese
Total Population: 124,800,000
Number of Children: 22,400,000
Favorite Sports: Baseball, soccer, and swimming
Environmental Fact: Tsukiji is the largest fish market in the world. Every day this market sells 2,500 tons of fish, which is more than the weight of 416 elephants.

Other "J" Countries: Jamaica and Jordan

Jambo (JAM-BO) from Kenya

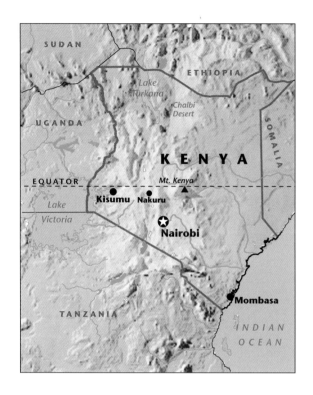

KENYA is home to many groups of people who have lived alongside each other for hundreds of years, speaking their own languages and finding different ways to make their living. The Kikuyu, for example, live in the highlands, where there is rain and cool weather, and grow coffee, tea, and corn on their farms. The people who live along the hot, wet coast grow coconuts and sugarcane and catch fish.

The Maasai live on the great plains of Kenya, where the land is very dry and good grass and water are hard to find. So they move from place to place with their cattle and goats, to make the most of what is there. Maasai children grow up drinking a lot of fresh, creamy milk and yogurt. They wear colorful bead necklaces and earrings—boys as well as girls, and old people as well as young people.

Most Kenyans live in the country, but about one-quarter of them live in towns like Nairobi, the capital. And like townspeople everywhere, they do things like repair cars, go to school, make or sell things, or work in offices or hotels. If you were going to a typical school in Kenya, you would wear a school uniform just like your classmates. The uniforms are often quite colorful.

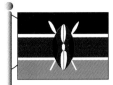

Many foreigners come to Kenya to see its famous game parks and beaches. You don't have to travel far from Nairobi to see giraffes, elephants, antelopes, lions, and rhinoceroses. There used to be plenty of land and water for all the people and the animals. But now there are many more humans, and people have to figure out how to share it all.

Kenyans like the idea of harambee, which means "all pull together." There are lots of other ways to have harambee. You can have fun with it by playing together, like the schoolchildren in the photos. And you can invent useful things from what is around you, like the boy pictured with his homemade bicycle.

More facts about Kenya

Capital: Nairobi

Languages: English, Swahili, and other African languages

Total Population: 27,300,000

Number of Children: 13,800,000

Favorite Sport: Soccer

Environmental Fact:
Kenyan women protect the environment by planting trees. They call it "Save the Land Harambee." Trees provide food, fuel, and medicine for people in rural Kenya. Over 12 million trees have been planted since 1977.

Other "K" Countries:
Kazakhstan, Kiribati, Kuwait, and Kyrgyzstan

Labas (LA-BAHS) from Lithuania

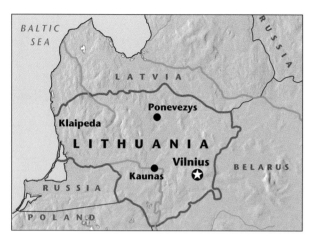

IF YOU were born before 1991, you are older than the new Lithuania. People have lived for a long time here, next to the Baltic Sea. For much of that time, neighboring nations ruled them. In this century, they were part of the Soviet Union. But in 1991, Lithuanians told the world that they wanted to be their own country, not part of a larger one.

Lithuania is so far north that in the winter there are only a few hours of daylight. But in the summer, the days are long and warm. Out in the country, farmers raise pigs and grow crops like wheat and potatoes, which thrive in Lithuania's rich, well-watered earth. It is a wide, gently rolling country with no mountains and has always been a good place for farming.

There is plenty to do outdoors in the summertime. In the city, children often take part in chalk-drawing competitions. These turn into community festivals, with people playing music to attract onlookers and make it more fun for everyone. You can also go waterskiing on one of Lithuania's three thousand lakes or steer a boat like the girl in the photograph, who is navigating along one of the 740 rivers in Lithuania.

Basketball is a game for all seasons, and Lithuanians are great fans of basketball. The country is very proud of its national team. The players are so good that their team has won many medals at the Olympic Games and several players now play on American professional teams.

Many Lithuanians are Christians belonging to the Roman Catholic Church. Like other Catholic children, when they are old enough to understand their faith, they take part in a

ceremony called First Communion. You can see how they dress up for this important occasion, with the girls in white dresses and the boys in colorful Lithuanian costumes.

More facts about Lithuania

Capital: Vilnius
Language: Lithuanian
Total Population: 3,700,000
Number of Children: 900,000
Favorite Sports: Basketball, soccer, and handball
Environmental Fact: Lithuanian children like to go out into the woods and fields in the summer and fall to pick wild mushrooms and berries. They are very careful only to pick ones that are safe to eat.

Other "L" Countries: Laos, Latvia, Lebanon, Lesotho, Liberia, Libya, Liechtenstein, and Luxembourg

Hola from Mexico

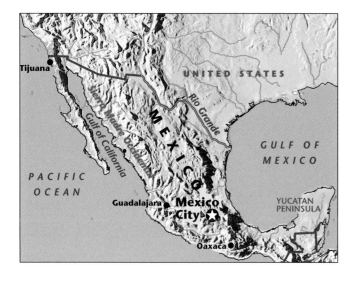

MANY children in Mexico live with members of their extended family, which includes themselves, their brothers and sisters, and their parents, as well as their aunts, uncles, cousins, and grandparents. The household will often come together for the comida—the main meal of the day.

Mexico has many different kinds of foods but nearly everyone eats beans, rice, and tortillas. Tortillas are made with flour, water, and cornmeal, and are shaped by hand into round, flat cakes. Meals with tortillas are a big part of Mexican celebrations, like el Día de los Muertos (the Day of the Dead).

The Day of the Dead is celebrated on November 2, a day that Christians remember all people who have died. In Mexico, everyone celebrates this holiday in a big way. Families get together and hang up fake skulls and skeletons, eat candy in the shape of bones, and decorate the graves where their relatives are buried with candles and flowers, just like in the photo. They spend the day with the dead, talking about them, praying, singing, and sharing food and drink.

Another big holiday is the Feast of the Virgin of Guadalupe. As the story goes, a local farmer saw Mary, the mother of Jesus, in the hills near Mexico City. People began to visit the site because it was a holy place. Now thousands of them come every year, and the feast is celebrated all over Mexico. Here you see children celebrating the feast in the town of Oaxaca.

You can also see some young boys playing in a fountain in Guadalajara. Guadalajara is Mexico's second-largest city and is so beautiful that it has been given a nickname: the Pearl of

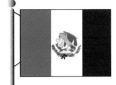

the West. Many Mexican children have to work hard every day, but like children all over the world, these boys have found a way to have fun, using what they find around them.

More facts about Mexico

Capital: Mexico City
Languages: Spanish and various Amerindian languages
Total Population: 91,900,000
Number of Children: 35,400,000
Favorite Sport: Soccer
Environmental Fact: Every fall, over 100 million black-and-orange monarch butterflies arrive to spend the winter in central Mexico's mountainous forests. These butterflies travel over 1,500 miles from the eastern and central parts of the United States.

Other "M" Countries:
Macedonia,
Madagascar,
Malawi,
Malaysia,
Maldives,
Mali, Malta,
Marshall Islands,
Mauritania,
Mauritius,
Micronesia,
Moldova,
Monaco,
Mongolia,
Morocco, and
Mozambique

Hello from Nigeria

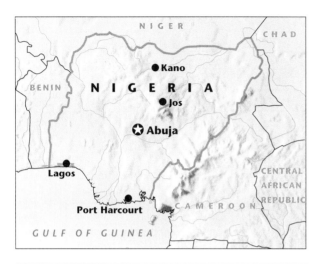

NIGERIA is a large country any way you measure it. If you tuned into the television or radio, you would hear the news broadcast in English and in all the country's major languages. Over four hundred languages are spoken here. Nigeria has more people than any other nation in Africa. It is blessed with good farmland and forest and oil, so it is also one of the wealthiest. And it stretches from sandy beaches in the south, through swamps and tropical forest, into dry grasslands where few trees grow. In the north, the land is almost desert.

About half the children in Nigeria go to primary school, and some go on to secondary school and university. The rest learn a trade at home. Like many other children in the world, they play alongside grown-ups as they work and learn by watching and helping where they can. Some will go out into the streets and sell things to passersby, like the boy on the next page who is selling peanuts in the town of Jos. Even small children will help in some way.

The women and children in another of the photographs are Igbo, from the east of Nigeria. The adults are decorating calabashes, which make good bowls and pots for storing or carrying things in. Calabashes are like pumpkins. When they dry out, you can carve patterns on the hard outside skin and scorch the patterns black with burnt sticks.

Wherever they live, Nigerians love to get together to celebrate special days. Maybe it is a child's first birthday. Or the farmers are harvesting their yams. Maybe it is the day of the masquerade, when someone puts on a huge

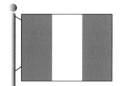

mask and dances around, while other people sing or beat on drums. If you are a good drummer, you can beat out high and low notes on the drums to make them sound like they are talking.

More facts about Nigeria

Capital: Abuja

Languages: English, Hausa, Yoruba, Ibo, Fulani, and other African languages

Total Population: 108,500,000

Number of Children: 51,800,000

Favorite Sport: Soccer

Environmental Fact: Nuts of the kola tree are crushed to make the juice used in cola drinks. When you give someone a kola nut, it is a sign of friendship.

Other "N" Countries: Namibia, Nauru, Nepal, Netherlands, New Zealand, Nicaragua, Niger, North Korea, and Norway

مَرْحَبًا (MAR-HA-BA) from Oman

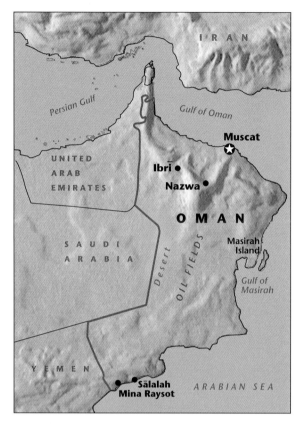

THE LEADER of Oman is Sultan Qaboos bin Said. When he came to power, he told his people that their country had once been famous and strong, and he would work to make it so again. Every Omani would play a part in reaching this goal.

If you go to Oman today, you can see how far the country has come, using the money it has earned from selling oil. Where before there were only rough tracks, now there are wide roads. Where children once might have gone blind from eye disease or been disabled by accidents or illness, there are now hospitals where they can get treatment.

When the parents of these children were little, there were only three schools in the whole country, and they were only for boys. Now there are over one thousand schools, for girls as well as boys. In fact, at the new university, there are more women students than men. And girls can look forward to growing up and getting interesting jobs like being an air traffic controller or a doctor.

There are 14,000 boy and girl scouts in Oman. The uniform for the girl scouts includes a head scarf, because that is the traditional dress for girls. On special occasions, girls will dress up and wear shimmering robes and decorate their hands with henna, which is a dye made from the flowers of a tree.

Half of Oman's people work in traditional jobs like farming and fishing. Some children know all about looking after sheep. Others are fish experts. You can see two boys throwing handfuls of sardines into a pile on the beach. Fishermen caught the sardines in the Arabian

Sea, brought them to land, and dumped them on the sand to dry out. These sardines will not be eaten, but turned into fertilizer for crops grown in the mountains and valleys of Oman.

More facts about Oman

Capital: Muscat

Languages: Arabic, English, Baluchi, and Urdu

Total Population: 2,100,000

Number of Children: 1,000,000

Favorite Sports: Cricket, basketball, hockey, swimming, and volleyball

Environmental Fact: On many of the protected beaches of Oman, people come to watch the green sea turtles, which come ashore at night to dig their nests and lay their eggs.

Other "O" Countries: none

Mabuhay (MAH-BOO-HI) from the Philippines

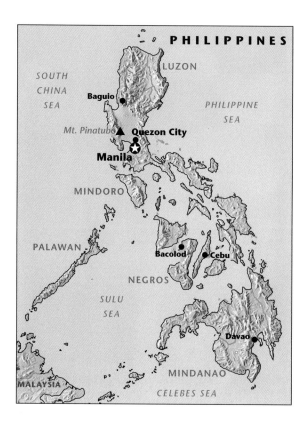

THE PHILIPPINES are a chain of over seven thousand islands in the Pacific Ocean. There are twelve large islands where most of the people live, but no Filipino lives very far from the sea.

Many different peoples live together in the Philippines. Some of them have been there so long, no one knows when or how they came. Others are more recent arrivals. The first European to come to the islands was the explorer Ferdinand Magellan, with three ships that barely made it across the Pacific. After him came the Spanish, who ruled the Philippines for over 350 years.

Through all this time, the Filipinos kept their own languages and many of their old customs. The girls in the photo on the next page are dancing to the music of gongs and bamboo flutes. They live in the north of Luzon, the largest island in the Philippines. Filipinos also learn a lot from people of other cultures. The boys on the next page are playing basketball, which is popular in the United States.

The children on the beach are lying down in what looks like mud, but in fact, it is clean black sand. The sand is black on the island of Luzon because it comes from volcanoes. The islands are made mostly from volcanoes: old, dead ones and new, active

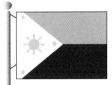

volcanoes that from time to time still send lava and ash spewing up into the air.

The young weaver lives on Mindanao, in the southern Philippines. She is weaving fabric on a loom, which keeps the long threads tight and lined up neatly. Many Filipinos are Christian, but on Mindanao, most people are Muslims. Filipino children, wherever they live and whatever their religion, always help their families by working or caring for their younger brothers and sisters.

More facts about the Philippines

Capital: Manila

Languages: Pilipino, also called Tagalog, English, and Philippine dialects

Total Population: 66,200,000

Number of Children: 27,000,000

Favorite Sport: Basketball

Environmental Fact: The Philippines are famous for handicrafts made from natural materials like bamboo and palm trees. These grow in great abundance and make excellent baskets and furnishings for people's houses.

Other "P" Countries: Pakistan, Palau, Panama, Papua New Guinea, Paraguay, Peru, Poland, and Portugal

مَرْحَبًا (MAR-HA-BA) from Qatar

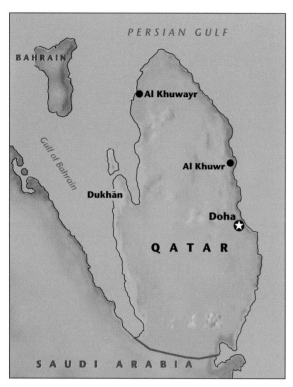

QATAR pokes out into the waters of the Persian Gulf like a big thumb, one hundred miles long and fifty miles wide. Although it has sea on three sides of it, the land is very dry because it gets very little rain. Qatar is mostly a flat, sandy desert. The shamal (a desert wind) can blow fierce sand and dust storms across the country.

One way that Qatar gets fresh water is by making it—in factories that take the salt out of seawater. Before they had these factories, the only way you could get a lot of water in Qatar was to pump it up from below the surface of the land or wait until winter, when some rain falls. There is just enough water for every day and to grow vegetables and raise sheep and goats.

Beneath the desert and the sandy bottom of the gulf are huge reserves of oil and natural gas that provide fuel for people's cars and buses and electricity for houses and factories. The government of Qatar sells this oil and gas to other nations and uses the money to build hospitals and parks and schools for its children.

Most Qatari are Muslims and carefully obey the rules set out in the Koran, their holy book. The boy in the picture on the next page is reading the Koran for his class in school. Children are taught that Muslims do not drink alcohol or wear showy clothes. They learn to pray five times a day and to go to a mosque for religious services. They treat their parents and elders with great respect.

Women and girls in Qatar dress modestly, often wearing a black robe (an abaya) over their clothes when they are in public. Girls like to go to the market with their mothers to shop. Boys

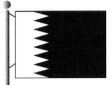

frequently play soccer with their fathers and brothers. Many families like to go to the desert or the beach for picnics. Whether you get together for fun or work or worship, your family is at the center of all you do.

More facts about Qatar

Capital: Doha

Languages: Arabic and English

Total Population: 534,000

Number of Children: 180,000

Favorite Sport: Soccer

Environmental Fact: Qatar has two farms where the white Arabian oryx is being bred for release into the wild. The legend of the unicorn may have evolved from travelers' descriptions of the white Arabian oryx.

Other "Q" Countries: none

Привет (PRI-VI-YET) from Russia

RUSSIA is the largest country in the world. Much of it lies north of the Arctic Circle, close to the North Pole. In the middle of summer, the sun shines all day and all night. This is the Land of the Midnight Sun, where the reindeer herders live.

Huge stretches of Russia are covered by forests, and you can go for hundreds of miles without coming across any villages or towns. The Khanty people, who have herded reindeer and hunted bear in these forests for hundreds of years, live in this part of Russia, often in log houses like the one you see in this photograph.

Most Russians have regular jobs in offices and factories, like grown-ups in other parts of the world. People tend to have small families. If you were Russian, you might have no brothers or sisters. But you would be very close to your grandparents, who would look after you while your parents worked.

Early this century, Russians fought bitterly for a new kind of government and persuaded or forced other countries to join them in one enormous country called the Soviet Union. They wanted to make life better for ordinary people, but in doing so, the people lost many basic freedoms. Now Russia is trying to change things. Twenty years ago, no one could have stood in the middle of the Red Square in Moscow and blown a shofar, like the boy in the

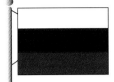

bottom photograph. (The shofar is made from a ram's horn and is used for important Jewish ceremonies.)

Despite the changes, some things are still the same, like fishing in Lake Baikal, or listening to a band playing in front of the Summer Palace in St. Petersburg.

More facts about Russia

Capital: Moscow

Languages: Russian and other Indo-European languages

Total Population: 147,400,000

Number of Children: 33,900,000

Favorite Sports: Basketball, gymnastics, track and field, skiing, soccer, and volleyball

Environmental Fact: Russia has the largest forest in the world. It is called the taiga and adds up to one-third of all the world's forest land. Most of the trees that grow there (like cedars, pines, spruces, and larches) have cones, which bear seeds for new trees.

Other "R" Countries: Romania and Rwanda

LIBERTY ELEMENTARY
SCHOOL LIBRARY

Bonjour from Senegal

IF YOU LIVED in Senegal, you would not get to climb any mountains, because there are none. Most of the country is gently rolling dry grassland, where people grow peanuts and millet and raise their sheep and cattle.

Millet is a grain, like wheat or oats, and is eaten every day all over Senegal. The two girls in the picture are pounding whole grains of millet into flour so that it can be boiled up into a porridge, just as oats can be cooked into oatmeal.

In one of the photographs, you see three boys having fun rolling old tires down the road. They have invented a game for themselves using things they found in the village.

Almost everyone in Senegal belongs to the religion known as Islam, whose followers are Muslims. Muslims believe in one God, called Allah. Like people of other religions, they have feasts and festivals. The smiling girl in the photo is all dressed up for one of them.

The most important holiday is Id al-Fitr. It celebrates the end of Ramadan, a month of quiet and prayer, when all Muslims—except for children or women who are expecting babies or people who are sick—will not eat or drink from sunup to sundown. On Id al-Fitr, children get presents, sweets, and colorful new clothes.

On the opposite page is a photo of a baptism. The baby is just seven days old, and a village elder bends close to the baby's head. He whispers her name into her ear three times. It is the first time the baby hears her name spoken. Next to the prayer mat is a bowl filled with kola nuts and millet. These things stand for blessings

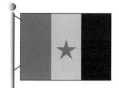

in Senegal and are given as gifts on special occasions like this one.

More facts about Senegal

Capital: Dakar

Languages: French, Wolof, and other African languages

Total Population: 8,100,000

Number of Children: 3,800,000

Favorite Sports: Soccer and wrestling

Environmental Fact: Seeds from the neem tree, originally from India, are ground up and soaked in water to form a mixture that is sprinkled on plants to kill insects without harming the environment.

Other "S" Countries: Saint Kitts and Nevis, Saint Lucia, Saint Vincent and the Grenadines, San Marino, Sao Tomé and Príncipe, Saudi Arabia, Serbia and Montenegro, Seychelles, Sierra Leone, Singapore, Slovakia, Slovenia, Solomon Islands, Somalia, South Africa, South Korea, Spain, Sri Lanka, Sudan, Suriname, Swaziland, Sweden, Switzerland, and Syria

Merhaba (MER-HA-BA) from Turkey

TURKEY is made up of seventy-three provinces, from Adana to Zonguldak. Many Turkish children grow up in modern cities, like the two boys from Istanbul that you see in this photograph. They are out on a fishing expedition, hoping to catch some fish.

The city of Istanbul is split down the middle by a strait of water called the Bosporus, where big ships sail up into the Black Sea or down into the Sea of Marmara, bearing trade goods and people, as they did in ancient times.

In one of the photographs, you can see some girls near a house that is built like a tent. The people who live in this region need homes that can be moved easily when they move their sheep to new pastures. So they make yurts, with strong poles and heavy cloth or animal skins sewn together.

Whatever kind of house people have, it is likely that they have rugs on the floor, and sometimes on the walls, too. The rug that you see hanging up for sale behind the boy and the motorcycle is called a kilim. Turkish carpets are among the finest in the world, and they are usually made by women in their homes. Older women teach children the different patterns and how to knot the wool into the backing fabric or weave them on looms.

Turkey is one of the few countries to have a national children's day. Every year, on April 23, schoolchildren dress up in traditional costumes and celebrate the day with dances and performances. Children from schools around the world are invited to take part. The festival is a nice break from regular school and a fun way to learn about the country and its past.

More facts about Turkey

Capital: Ankara

Languages: Turkish, Kurdish, and Arabic

Total Population: 60,800,000

Number of Children: 21,900,000

Favorite Sports: Soccer and wrestling

Environmental Fact: In the central part of Turkey, the land of Cappadocia is made of soft volcanic rock from which strange cone-shaped hills called fairy chimneys have formed.

Other "T" Countries: Tajikistan, Tanzania, Thailand, Togo, Tonga, Trinidad and Tobago, Tunisia, Turkmenistan, and Tuvalu

Hello from the United States

THE UNITED STATES OF AMERICA is one country made up of many peoples. In the schools of many cities, you see children who look like they come from China or Zimbabwe, Russia or Ecuador. There are Buddhists in the United States, as well as Christians, Hindus, Jews, and Muslims. You might sample food from India or France or hear the music of Brazil or Nigeria. You can buy clothes made of fabrics from Guatemala or Senegal. And you can also find things that are distinctly American, like jazz and pumpkin pie and baseball.

Every child in the United States hears stories of brave women and men who helped to make their country what it is today. Native American children, for example, tell stories about their ancestors, who lived here many of thousands of years before the new Americans came. Everyone can feel proud of some special thing that their ancestors shared with other Americans—from how to pop corn or print books like this one, to what it means for people to be free and equal.

In the photographs, you see some of these American children. There are three girls sharing a secret and two children taking a break from baseball practice. One boy is playing an imaginary clarinet, and another is getting a lesson from his grandfather on how to play a guitar. The children holding hands are learning a rabbit dance that their parents and grandparents learned when they were children.

The United States is huge, and most of its fifty states are bigger than some of the countries in this book. On one side lies the Pacific Ocean, on the other, the Atlantic. In between, you could

pick what kind of weather and landscape you like best and move there. With hope and hard work and a little luck, you can be anything you want to be and live anywhere you want—from A to Z—in the United States of America.

More facts about the United States

Capital: Washington, D.C.

Languages: English, Spanish, and Native American languages

Total Population: 260,600,000

Number of Children: 60,900,000

Favorite Sports: Basketball, baseball, football, and soccer

Environmental Fact: The first national park in the world is the Yellowstone National Park, in the Rocky Mountains. It is famous for its 200 geysers of hot water that spout up out of the ground to great heights. The biggest geyser is called Old Faithful and shoots 150 feet in the air once every hour.

Other "U" Countries: Uganda, Ukraine, United Arab Emirates, United Kingdom, Uruguay, and Uzbekistan

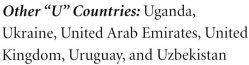

Xin Chào (SEEN-CHOW) from Vietnam

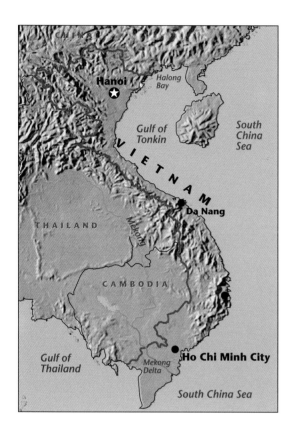

MANY CHILDREN in Vietnam go to school until they are about fifteen years old. The school day is short because many of the children also spend time helping their families at home or in the fields or by working to earn some money for the family. The young girl to your right is weaving reed baskets in the village of Lam Dien. She and her family will sell them at market.

In one of the photographs, you see children from the village of Phu Vinh who have gathered to greet some travelers. Many years after the Vietnam War ended in 1973, visitors began returning to the country and rebuilding friendships with the Vietnamese people.

The girl on the opposite page is waving to some friends swimming in the Mekong River, the longest river in Southeast Asia. Because much of Vietnam is mountainous, many people live in the lowlands of the Mekong Delta. The river washes down so much sand and silt that they collect and fan out at the river's mouth, where it meets the sea. This is how a delta is formed and how the Mekong Delta got its name. If you lived there, you might have a river house. River houses are built on stilts to keep them above water. Or your house might be a boat, floating on the river.

The delta is a perfect place to grow rice, which needs a lot of water to start growing. Women plant the rice in flooded fields called paddies. When the rice is

ready to harvest, it looks like tall grass. Vietnamese children in this part of the country eat rice at every meal, including breakfast.

Often there will be fish to eat with the rice. These children in Halong Bay have tied hooks on to lines and dropped them into the water. They are waiting for fish to come and nibble the bait dangling beneath their boat.

More facts about Vietnam

Capital: Hanoi

Languages: Vietnamese, French, Chinese, English, and Khmer

Total Population: 72,900,000

Number of Children: 29,100,000

Favorite Sports: Badminton and soccer

Environmental Fact: Vietnamese fishermen are some of the best in the world at catching shellfish, like crabs, shrimp, and lobsters. Lobsters grow in great numbers off the south coast of Vietnam.

Other "V" Countries: Vanuatu and Venezuela

Talofa (TA-LO-FA) from Western Samoa

LIFE IN Western Samoa revolves around the family, or aiga. Your aiga includes everyone who is even distantly related to you, and the more people there are in your aiga, the more important it is. The head of your aiga could be your grandmother or your uncle or your own father. She or he will also help run things in your village.

Everything in the village is kept clean and tidy. Of course, the children help, like the girl in the picture who is washing clothes. The government has a competition every year and awards prizes to the villages they think are the neatest and best cared for.

Children get plenty of time to have fun, swimming in the sea or playing at sports. Western Samoans love cricket and rugby. Children often make their own toys, like the two boys holding a toy outrigger canoe that they have made.

Most children wear lava lavas for clothing. These are long pieces of cloth that children (and adults) wear wrapped around their waists. A lava lava can be worn as a skirt, a dress, a bathing suit, and pajamas. They are light and cool and easy to wash.

You do not have to go to school in Western Samoa, but almost all children do. The last day of school is a day for giving out prizes and making speeches. You can see a girl and her mother dancing together for the occasion.

Every year on the second Sunday in October, Western Samoa honors its children. This day is called White Sunday because the people dress up in their best white clothes and go to church and sing hymns together. Then they go home to

open presents and eat fresh fruits and roasted pig.

More facts about Western Samoa

Capital: Apia

Languages: Samoan and English

Total Population: 163,000

Number of Children: 85,000

Favorite Sports: Kirikiti (cricket), netball, rugby, soccer, and volleyball

Environmental Fact: Because the weather in Western Samoa is hot and humid, traditional Samoan houses have no walls, in order to take advantage of the cool sea breezes.

Other "W" Countries: none

Welcome to Xanadu

Xanadu is an imaginary country. It is a place where you can be who you want to be. In Xanadu people laugh, dance, and sing. They listen to each other and work together to solve problems. In Xanadu it doesn't matter what you look like or where you come from; you will always have friends. Students at Forest View Elementary School in Durham, North Carolina, in the United States of America, have painted a gigantic ten-foot-by-ten-foot mural of Xanadu, which you can see on the opposite page. Here are some of the things they said about their imaginary country:

Xanadu is a place of peace and love. Where people will respect you and love you. A perfect place to live is a sunflower house. Where music follows you along the way.—*Jasmina Nogo*

Xanadu would be very nice. There would be no fighting. There would be love. Everybody would share and no robberies. There would be enough food. There would be nothing like money and no starving. I would like people to love each other not hate. I would not like pollution or trash. I wish there was this place on this planet. I'd stay all my life.—*Seo Kim*

To live in Xanadu an imaginary country is to be surfboarding and to see people getting off a boat, reading, walking a dog, playing hand games, picking flowers. It is a perfect place to live.—*Emily Lytle*

In Xanadu no one is rich and no one is poor. In a town in Xanadu everyone is kind. In a town in Xanadu there is no fighting, and there are no guns or weapons.—*Cassady Burke*

In Xanadu my house is a two-floored house. The attic has a long window. It belongs to a chief. His moose is having a good time. He is sleeping till 9:00 A.M. He has a letter in his mailbox.—*Anjan Mukherjee*

The perfect place to live is under the bed. It's in the dark. You can eat cookies all day. And drink Kool-Aid.—*Sophie Bell*

More facts about Xanadu

Capital: Imagination City

Languages: Kindness and Respect

Total Population: Everyone who wants to live in an imaginary country.

Number of Children: All children who dream of a better world.

Favorite Sports: All fun games and activities that can be played on water, land, or in the air.

Environmental Facts: The air and water are perfectly clean. There is no pollution and no garbage. Everything can be recycled or reused.

Other "X" countries: none

Xanadu is a place where there's flowers and there's no violence and it's quiet and it's a peaceful place.
That's a place for you and me.—*Latia Ward*

مَرْحَبًا (MAR-HA-BA) from Yemen

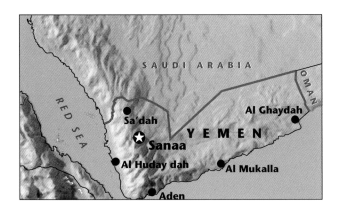

THE CAPITAL CITY of Yemen is Sanaa, in the northwest of the country. The buildings there are tall and white and have stained-glass windows. The white paint reflects the blazing sunlight and helps keep the buildings cool all day.

Not much rain falls in Yemen, especially along the coast. There are no streams or rivers that flow all year. The animals that do best in very dry areas are, of course, camels, like the one the little girl is holding on to in the picture.

Camels aren't fussy about what kind of grass they get, and they can go a long time between meals. If you are lucky, you might see a camel in Yemen, but nowadays most people use trucks or donkeys.

The boys standing in a row are showing off some toy trucks they have made. They used old plastic jugs and cans for the bodies and circles cut from old flip-flops for the wheels.

Most Yemeni are Muslims. There are lots of differences among Muslim countries, but in many of them girls and women will cover their hair when they are out of doors, like the girls in these photographs.

One photograph shows a girl standing with her brother in front of a wall. Her hands are painted with henna in a good luck pattern. It will wash off after a few weeks. Yemeni women and girls like to decorate their hands with different patterns for special occasions, like birthdays, weddings, and feast days.

When boys want to wear something special, they might wear a curved knife called a jambia. Knives like these were once used as weapons, but now they are for decoration and to show that you come from an important family.

More facts about Yemen

Capital: Sanaa

Language: Arabic

Total Population: 13,900,000

Number of Children: 6,800,000

Favorite Sports: Cricket and soccer

Environmental Fact: Farmers dig out the sides of the mountains to create small, level plots called terraces. Enough rain falls in the mountains to grow plants like coffee, millet, bananas, and papayas.

Other "Y" Countries: none

Mahoroi (MA-HAY-ROY) from Zimbabwe

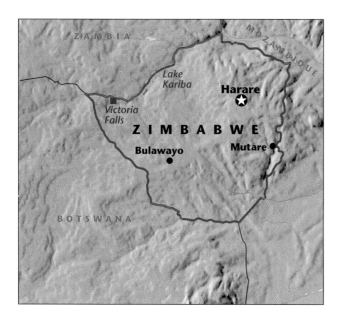

A LONG TIME AGO, people in this part of Africa built a large city, which they called Zimbabwe. The name means "stone houses." When the people of this country were looking for a new name for their nation, they chose this old one, which reminds them of their long and proud history.

If you travel around Zimbabwe today, you will see a lot of stone. Huge stone boulders the size of office buildings lie scattered over the land, some of them balancing on smaller ones, like elephants doing tricks at a circus.

Millions of Zimbabwians live in cities and towns. But most families live in the country and work on farms, tending cows and growing corn or cotton. Usually, the year divides into two seasons: one wet and the other dry. If enough rain falls in the rainy season, the farms do well. But some years, there is not much rain at all. Children who live in the countryside know how much their families depend on the weather.

Visitors come from far and wide to take photographs of the wild elephants, buffalo, and antelopes that live here. The parents of many children earn their living by providing the tourists with what they need for their safaris: hotels and places to shop, guides and car drivers and mechanics. The money that tourists spend helps the country in many ways.

With some help from the government, a town might build a clinic, so if a child is sick, the parents do not have to travel for miles and miles to find a doctor. Or people might make bricks from the local clay and build a school, like the one you see in the photograph.

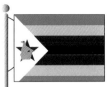

Children figure out ways to use what is around them. The boy in the photograph wanted a guitar. But ready-made guitars cost a lot of money. So he found some wood and made one for himself.

More facts about Zimbabwe

Capital: Harare

Languages: Shona, English, and Sindebele

Total Population: 11,000,000

Number of Children: 5,100,000

Favorite Sports: Cricket, netball, and soccer

Environmental Fact: The Victoria Falls are one of the seven natural wonders of the world. In Zimbabwe, they are called mosi-oa-tunya, or "the smoke that thunders."

Other "Z" Countries: Zambia

Afterword

Now that you have finished reading and learning from the photographs of *Children from Australia to Zimbabwe: A Photographic Journey around the World,* I hope you will feel a part of and connected to a much larger community— the community of the world's children. For just as we are citizens of our own countries, we are also citizens of the world. You can continue to learn about people and other countries all your life. Here are some ideas on how you can truly be a global citizen:

• Look for books about children living in other communities. Some of my favorites are *Children Just Like Me* by Barnabas and Anabel Kindersley, *Come with Me to Africa* by Gregory Scott Kreikemeier, and *Far North,* in the Vanishing Culture Series, by Jan Reynolds. They should be in your local library.

• Become a member of a pen pal club and write letters to your new friend in a different country. The Internet is a new and easy way to write letters to children from many different parts of the world.

• Find music from different countries that you can listen and dance to. One of my favorite recordings is *Reggae for Kids.* Originally from Jamaica, reggae music uses strong drumbeats.

• Learn a new word in a different language every day. For example, if you are interested in learning French or Hindi or Spanish or Swahili, learn a new word every day from that language. Ask family friends or school friends to teach you, or check your local library for picture dictionaries or books in that language.

• If you have classmates from other countries, ask questions to learn more about them and the country where they are from.

• Eat food from a different country in a restaurant or in your own home. Check out a children's cookbook from the library and make dishes from a variety of countries.

• Find out what countries vegetables, flowers, or plants originally came from.

• When you go to the store, look for labels on food or clothes or toys. If they are made outside your country, find out more about the country where they are made.

• If you have the opportunity to visit a new country, go! There are some student exchange programs that start with kids who are eleven years old.

• Draw your own Xanadu and write down your ideas of an imaginary country.

There is a famous saying, "Think globally, act locally." I encourage you to "Think globally, act locally *and* globally." No matter how old you are, try to help other children, whether it is your friend, a classmate, or a child that lives halfway across the world. As a global citizen,

you are responsible for making this world a better place to live for future generations.

—MAYA K. AJMERA

If you have other ideas of how to be a global citizen, or if you have created your own Xanadu, write to us and share:

Global Citizenship Project
P.O. Box 99350, Duke Station
Durham, NC 27708

Forest View Elementary School students—Omayra Lema, top; Kyle Griffen, left; Simon Gaddy, right; and Manuela Navarro, middle—have become part of their imaginary country, Xanadu.

Acknowledgments

Children from Australia to Zimbabwe, A Photographic Journey around the World is a project of S H A K T I for Children. Evoking the Hindi word for empowerment, S H A K T I for Children is a nonprofit organization that teaches children to value diversity and grow into productive, caring citizens of the world.

After returning from a trip to Mexico, photographer Steve Macauley said, "I think I have captured some S H A K T I moments!" This book is full of such moments. In all, we received over 1,700 photographs of children from countries across the alphabet, from Australia to Zimbabwe. The bulk of the photographs were received from Peace Corps volunteers. Whether they were amateur or professional photographers, the commitment of these individuals to global citizenship breathed life into this project. Without their photographs, there would be no *Children from Australia to Zimbabwe*.

Photographers: Byron Augustin, Mark Beach, Mike Bell, Tom Bolin, World Bank/Curt Carnemark, Stephen Chicoine, Margaret Courtney-Clarke, Pablo Corral, Cecil Cole, Patrick Colquhoun, Kimberly Cupp, Richard A. Foster, Steven G. Herbert, Patricia Heydorn, Jack Hillmeyer, Rachel Isaacson, John D. Ivanko, Laurel Iverson, Ian James, Maureen Johnson, Catherine Karnow, Zinas Kazenas, Anne Keiser, Patty Kelley/World Vision, Thomas L. Kelly, Katharine Kimball, David Kramer, Gregory Scott Kreikemeier, Gray Laughridge/Wilmington Star News, Steve Lehman/SABA, Jennifer Leonard, Paula Lerner, Chuck Liddy/News and Observer, Elaine Little, Richard Lobell/United Jewish Appeal, Steve Macauley, Rachel Miksad, James Miller, Emily Nolte, Ellen O'Donnell, Ania D. Porazinski, Jan Reynolds, G. L. Scarfiotti/ARAMCO World, Linda Schaefer/Impact Visuals, Lynn Simarski/ARAMCO WORLD, Sean Sprague, Snook Stratakos, William Tracy/ARAMCO WORLD, Monte VanDeusen, Delores Walters, Bernard Wolf/Monkmeyer, and Lark Worth. Other organizations provided guidance and photographs: AMIDEAST, Balzekas Museum of Lithuanian Culture, Brady Lambert Photography, Catholic Relief Services, embassies of Australia, Ecuador, Lithuania, and Oman, Mennonite Central Committee, Peace Corps of America, Plan International, SERRV International, and UNICEF.

The Xanadu Project was a remarkable collaboration between S H A K T I for Children and Forest View Elementary School in Durham, North Carolina. Forest View Elementary was a perfect match for this project as the school has students with ties to 41 countries. Coordinating the project was Vanessa Davis of S H A K T I for Children and art teacher Marylu Flowers-Schoen at Forest View Elementary. This book not only celebrates children from around the world but also celebrates the creativity of the 1995–1996 third- and third/fourth-grade multiaged classes and their vision for a better world.

Students: Rashad Aldridge, Gerald Alston, Marcus Anderson, Eric Arendshorst, Ruth Attamack, Alloray Baker, Alphonso Barnes, Allison Bartlett, Germaine Baugh, Jamie Bell, Sophie Bell, Joshua Bennetone, Darius Rorie-Blackmon, Jesica Bonilla, Kalynn Botts, Christopher Breeden, Christopher Briggs, Charlene Broomes, Jeffrey Brown, Patrick Brown, Audrina Bunton, Cassady Burke, Matthew Clayton, Sean Clayton, William Clayton, Joshua Climer, Marlo Cohen, Charlissa Copeland, Marcus Cousin, Robert Crumpler, Christopher Dadok, Du Dai, Johnny Dang, Shavon Daniel, Taijia Dennis, Bethany Diprete, Sara Dodson, Barrett Donner, Emelia Dunston, Elise Edgerton, Mandel Edwards, Sirgeo Ellis, Yvette Eregie, Jay-ar Foronda, Molly Freeman, Emily Frenzel, Simon Gaddy, Jesse Gellerson, Gregory Gibson, Bettina Goesele, Jennifer Gore, Zachary Gornto, Ta'shanna Gray, Niketa Green, Kyle Griffin, Jessica Hackett, Tyler Harris, Darrell Harris, Tequila Harris, Brittany Hayes, Jessica Henderson, Damon Henry, Sade Henry, Abigail Hernandez, Dante Hill, Alexandria Horne, Paul Huang, Hanna Hwang, Bryce Jenkins, Sabrina Jennette, Katherine Johnston, Jasmyne Jones, Dallas Kegley, Grace Kendall, Jamahl Kennard, Aditya Kher, Seo Kim, Jonathan Lampe, Bilal Lateef, Omayra Lema, Benjamin Leone, Jason Leone, Janice Liu, Syrone Liu, Bryan Lochman, Judithe Louis, Mariam Loynab, Emily Lytle, Brandon Madden, Mary Jane Martin, Hector Maya, Lauren McAskill, Kim McCallum, Sean McCauley, Kempest McEachirn, Rowan Meehan, Lydia Mikhaylyants, Emily Miller, Kathryn Mims, Brian Moran, Anjan Mukherjee, Saif Murad, Randell Murrell, Manuela Navarro, Jasmina Nogo, Alicia Oas, Natishia O'Neal,

Onunga Ooro, Ezinne Oputa, Michelle Ostrowski, Jarrell Peak, Kevin Pearlstein, Travis Peele, Nicholas Philbrick, Christina Quintano, Brandon Rabb, Erik Ramires, Joshua Rivera, Natalie Rossman, Donald Rush, Dylan Russell, Danna Saleh, Taylor Savage, Karthik Sekar, Anastassia Sharpe, Kevin Shumaker, Jesse Shumate, Jeffrey Smith, Solomon Tate, Mario Tedder, Kendra Tee, Abdramane Traore, Natalie Turkaly, Kissel Valencia, Samuel Valencia, Jose Velazquez, Claire Walker, Andre Ward, Latia Ward, Whitney Wicker, Adriene Williams, Jason Williams, Tishonda Williams, Shamecka Williamson, Evan Witkowski, Hayley Wood, Teshana Young, and Chenwei Zhang. In addition, thanks to Toni Hill, principal; Sandy Lyles, media specialist; third- and third/fourth-grade multiage teachers and teacher assistants; Anne Occor, ESL teacher; and the Forest View Elementary School PTA.

Children from Australia to Zimbabwe is grateful to the **echoing green** Foundation and the Z. Smith Reynolds Foundation for providing the institutional support needed to make this dream come true. The support for research, development, and test marketing was provided by American Express, the Association for the Promotion of International Cooperation in Japan, Body Shop USA Foundation, Mary Reynolds Babcock Foundation, Mary Duke Biddle Foundation, the Durham Merchants' Association Charitable Foundation, Imaginations Unlimited, the North Carolina Arts Council/National Endowment for the Arts, R & M Enterprises, the Versola family, and anonymous donors and foundations. In-kind support was provided by the Center for International Development Research at the Terry Sanford Institute of Public Policy, Duke University, and Moore & Van Allen, PLLC of Durham, NC.

In 1996, every K-5 public elementary school in North Carolina received three copies of *Children from Australia to Zimbabwe*. This effort was supported by the N.C. Department of Cultural Resources and by North Carolina's thriving philanthropic community: American Airlines' Kids are Something Special Fund of the Triangle Community Foundation, American Express, Bell South, Body Shop USA Foundation, Cannon Foundation, Carolina Power & Light, Duke Power Company Foundation, Charlotte World Affairs Council, Grace Jones Richardson Trust, IBM, Reichhold Chemicals, RR Donnelley & Sons Company, Sprint Mid-Atlantic, Teddie and Tony Brown Fund, Z. Smith Reynolds Foundation, and many individual friends and anonymous supporters.

The core individuals involved in this project were director, Maya Ajmera; coauthor, Anna Rhesa Versola; community outreach coordinators, Vanessa Davis and N.C. Public Ally Olateju S. Omolodun; editor, Maura High; research assistants, Susan Beale, Greg Davis, and Ginger Norwood; consultants, Lisa Daughtry, Jodi Detjen, and Derek Sappenfield; Hart leadership team, Annette DeNoyer and Linda Kane. We are also indebted to Anne Theilgard and Joyce Kachergis of Kachergis Book Design. In late 1994, Marian Wright Edelman embraced this vision, having only a very rough sketch of the book. We are thankful to Mrs. Edelman and Donna Jablonski of the Children's Defense Fund. The present and former boards of directors of S H A K T I for Children provided the guidance and support for this project: William Ascher, Anthony Brown, Amy Chua, Laura Luger, Tom McCarty, Adele Richardson Ray, Jason Schultz, and Christopher Welna.

Maya Ajmera thanks her family and loved ones and personal friends who provided enormous support during the two years it took to make the book. Anna Rhesa Versola would like especially to thank Eddie Kallam, her husband, and her parents, Manuel and Mila Versola, for their encouragement and inspiration to pursue high ideals. Vanessa Davis thanks her family and friends for their love and support.

In 1994 *Children from Australia to Zimbabwe* was just the idea of one person. What has transpired since then was a remarkable coming together of individuals, groups, and organizations to contribute their wisdom, talents, and resources to this project. They all became Friends of Children from Australia to Zimbabwe. Martin Luther King Jr. once said, "If you want to move people, it has to be toward a vision that's positive for them, that taps important values, that gets them something they desire, and it has to be presented in a compelling way that they feel inspired to follow." Now that the movement has begun, *Children from Australia to Zimbabwe* will be the centerpiece of our vision.

🐛 In honor of their commitment to family,
friends, and community

Linda A. Ironside (1964–1995)
Prakash C. Jain (1939–1987)
Rippan Kapur (1954–1994)
Vineeta Rastogi (1968–1995)
Joel Sondak (1932–1995)

M. K. A.

Copyright © 1997 by SHAKTI for Children
Original copyright © 1996 and publication 1996 by SHAKTI for Children
Foreword copyright © 1996 by the Children's Defense Fund
Afterword copyright © 1996 by Maya Ajmera

Developed by SHAKTI for Children
Box 99350, Duke Station, Durham, North Carolina 27708

Published by Charlesbridge Publishing
85 Main Street, Watertown, Massachusetts 02172
(617)926-0329

Population figures were obtained from *The State of the World's Children 1996*, UNICEF.

We are grateful to the many people who contributed to this book. Any errors that remain in the book are the responsibility of the authors.

Photographs: left to right, counterclockwise: **Front Book Jacket Cover:** © International Public Affairs Branch of the Australian DFAT; © Gregory Scott Kreikemeier; © International Public Affairs Branch of the Australian DFAT. **Back Book Jacket Cover:** © Ania D. Porazinski. **Half Title Page:** © Steve Macauley. **Title Page:** © Zinas Kazenas; © Jack Hillmeyer; © John D. Ivanko. **Foreword:** © Elaine Little. **Australia:** © International Public Affairs Branch of the Australian DFAT; © International Public Affairs Branch of the Australian DFAT; © International Public Affairs Branch of the Australian DFAT; © Jan Reynolds. **Brazil:** © Linda Schaefer/Impact Visuals; © Thomas L. Kelly; © Ania D. Porazinski; © Sean Sprague/Catholic Relief Services 1993. **China:** © Jack Hillmeyer; © Paula Lerner; © Mike Bell; © World Bank/Curt Carnemark. **Dominican Republic:** © Tom Bolin; © Patrick Colquhoun; © Katharine Kimball; © Tom Bolin. **Ecuador:** © Pablo Corral; © Gregory Scott Kreikemeier; © John D. Ivanko; © John D. Ivanko. **France:** © Catherine Karnow; © Catherine Karnow; © Maya Ajmera; © Catherine Karnow. **Guatemala:** © Steve Macauley; © Patrick Colquhoun; © Patrick Colquhoun; © Kimberly Cupp. **Hungary:** (all photographs) © Sean Sprague. **India:** © John D. Ivanko; © Maya Ajmera; © Steve Macauley; Sean Sprague/Catholic Relief Services 1993. **Japan:** © Paula Lerner; © Elaine Little; © Ian James; © Ian James. **Kenya:** © Snook Stratakos; © Mark Beach; © Sean Sprague/Catholic Relief Services 1993; © Sean Sprague/Catholic Relief Services 1993. **Lithuania:** © Zinas Kazenas; © Stephen Chicoine; © Zinas Kazenas; © Zinas Kazenas. **Mexico:** © Bernard Wolf/Monkmeyer; © Steve Macauley; © Sean Sprague; © Bernard Wolf/Monkmeyer. **Nigeria:** © Monte VanDeusen; © Margaret Courtney-Clarke; © Cecil Cole. **Oman:** © Information Attaché, Embassy of Oman; © James Miller; © William Tracy/ARAMCO World; © Lynn Simarski/ARAMCO World. **Philippines:** © Jennifer Leonard; © Elaine Little; © Elaine Little; © Elaine Little. **Qatar:** © Byron Augustin; © Byron Augustin; © G. L. Scarfiotti/ARAMCO World; © Byron Augustin. **Russia:** © Stephen Chicoine; © Richard Lobell/United Jewish Appeal; © Anne Keiser; © Sean Sprague. **Senegal:** © Steven Herbert; © Emily Nolte; © Ellen O'Donnell; © Laural Iverson. **Turkey:** © Jan Reynolds; © Jan Reynolds; © David Kramer; © Jan Reynolds. **United States:** © Catherine Karnow; © Gray Laughridge/Wilmington Star News; © Catherine Karnow; © Steve Lehman/ SABA; © Catherine Karnow. **Vietnam:** © Richard A. Foster; © Rachel Isaacson; © Richard A. Foster; © Rachel Isaacson. **Western Samoa:** ©Anne Keiser; © Maureen Johnson; © Maureen Johnson; © Rachel Miksad. **Xanadu:** © 1995–1996 Forest View Elementary, third-grade and third/ fourth-grade combination classes and SHAKTI for Children, Durham, NC, U.S.A. **Yemen:** © Patricia Heydorn; © Delores Walters; © Patricia Heydorn; © Delores Walters. **Zimbabwe:** © Lark Worth; © World Vision/Patty Kelley; © World Vision/Patty Kelley; © Gregory Scott Kreikemeier. **Afterword:** © John D. Ivanko; © Chuck Liddy/News and Observer.

All rights reserved under the International and Pan-American Copyright Convention. This book, or parts thereof, may not be reproduced in any form without permission from the publisher.

This book was designed and produced by Kachergis Book Design, Pittsboro, North Carolina.

This book was printed in Reynosa, Mexico, by RR Donnelley & Sons Company.

10 9 8 7 6 5 4 3 2 1

LIBRARY OF CONGRESS CATALOGING-IN-PUBLICATION DATA
Ajmera, Maya.
    Children from Australia to Zimbabwe: a photographic journey around the world/Maya Ajmera & Anna Rhesa Versola; with a foreword by Marian Wright Edelman.
        p.   cm.
    Originally published: Durham, N.C.: SHAKTI for Children, © 1996.
    Summary: Text and photographs depict how children live in nations across the alphabet, from Australia to Zimbabwe.
    ISBN 0-88106-999-x (hc)
    1. Human geography—Juvenile literature. 2. Children—Juvenile literature. 3. Human geography—Pictorial works—Juvenile literature. 4. Children—Pictorial works—Juvenile literature. [1. Human geography. 2. Alphabet.] I. Versola, Anna Rhesa. II. Title.
GF48.A45   1997
305.23[E]   97-12254

LIBERTY ELEMENTARY SCHOOL

WITHDRAWN

3 6414 00591446 1   305.23 AJM
Children from Australia to

LIBERTY ELEMENTARY SCHOOL

3 6414 00591446 1   305.23 AJM
Children from Australia to